NIC BISHOP
FROGS

scholastic 💡 nonfiction
an imprint of

SCHOLASTIC

Blue dart poison frog

The author wishes to thank the Binder Park Zoo.

Copyright © 2008 by Nic Bishop.
All rights reserved. Published by Scholastic Inc.
SCHOLASTIC, SCHOLASTIC NONFICTION, and associated logos
are trademarks and/or registered trademarks of Scholastic Inc.

LIBRARY OF CONGRESS CATALOGING-IN-PUBLICATION DATA
Bishop, Nic, 1955– • Nic Bishop frogs. • p. cm. • Includes index.
1. Frogs—Juvenile literature. • I. Title. • QL668.E2B47 • 2008 •
597.8'9—dc22 • 2007008699

ISBN 13: 978-0-439-87755-8 • ISBN 10: 0-439-87755-5

10 9 8 7 6 5   10 11 12

Printed in Singapore 46 • First printing, January 2008
Book design by Nancy Sabato

African bullfrog

The frog on the title page is a bumblebee dart poison frog

For Emma and Laura
— N. B.

Red-eyed tree frog

FROGS are found on every continent except Antarctica.

They live in ponds, rivers, forests, and fields. Some even live in sand dunes.

The biggest, the Goliath frog from Africa, is as heavy as a newborn baby. One of the smallest, the gold frog from South America, could sit on the tip of your little finger. But, big or small, frogs are always easy to recognize. Almost all have long back legs, a large head, big eyes, damp stretchy skin, and no tails.

Frogs are amphibians, which means they lead "two lives," in water and on land. Many live near ponds and swamps, like this growling grass frog from Australia.

Some people are confused about the difference between a frog and a toad, but you do not have to be. A toad is just a kind of frog. It usually has drier skin than other frogs and can live farther from water. It also has shorter legs, so it hops rather than jumps.

Toads can live a long time.

A pet toad in England was famous for living for thirty-six years. A bullfrog, by comparison, may live for about twenty years in captivity.

Toads are often found in forests or even in backyards. Some people think they look ugly, but toads can produce the most beautiful trilling calls during springtime.

Most frogs are found near ponds, swamps, and other wet places.

They need water, but they do not drink it. Instead, they absorb it through their skin, even just when sitting on damp ground.

And that's not all. Although frogs have lungs, they breathe through their skin, too. A frog can breathe more than half of the oxygen it needs through its skin, but only if the skin is damp. A frog must never dry out or it will suffocate. Naturally, frogs like to look after their special skin. To do this, they shed it every so often. They wriggle and arch their backs to split the old skin and roll it off. Then they usually eat it!

Most frogs have large eyes on top of their head so they can see all around and watch for predators. This African bullfrog is a baby. You can see how it looks as an adult on page 40.

Frog skin comes in every color, and can even be see-through. Look at the insides of the glass frog in this photograph. You can see the heart that pumps blood, as well as the stomach and intestines that digest food. Frogs have organs similar to yours.

Frogs have bones like you, too, but not as many. While adult humans have 206 bones, frogs have about 159. So they are missing some. Frogs, for example, do not have rib bones. That is one reason they are so good at squeezing through small gaps, like between your fingers when you are trying to hold them.

Glass frogs are good climbers. They live in trees and bushes, in the rain forests of Central and South America. Nobody really knows why their skin is transparent.

About half of a frog's bones are in its feet, which can wiggle and grip things almost like hands. These feet help their owners in wonderful ways. Frogs that live near water often have webbed hind feet for swimming. Frogs that burrow in the ground, such as spadefoot toads, can have clawlike spades on their hind feet for digging.

Tree frogs have feet for climbing.

Each toe has a sucker at the tip which holds fast to leaves and branches. Red-eyed tree frogs can even hang upside down by their toes.

Frogs are always alert to their surroundings. They have good senses of taste and touch. They can hear well, too, although you have to look hard to see their ears. Each is a circle of skin, called a *tympanum*, just behind the eye. The tympanum vibrates like a drum skin when sound hits it, and this sends a signal to the brain.

The red-eyed tree frog wakes up at dusk to hunt for insects in rain forest trees in Central America. When it sleeps during the day, it tucks its toes under its green body and shuts its eyes, to look like a green leaf.

A frog's eyes are large and quick to spot movement. Anything that wriggles is inspected. If it looks tasty, the frog gets ready to pounce.

Most frogs use their tongues to catch prey. **The tongue is coated with sticky mucus and shoots forward with deadly aim to snatch prey and toss it back into the mouth.** Then the frog may use its eyes again, this time to swallow the prey whole. It blinks both eyeballs down toward its mouth where they help push the prey into its stomach.

This frog's tongue is joined to the front part of the mouth so it can flip out a long way to grab a caterpillar.

A frog's life is all about eating.

Frogs eat almost anything that moves and can fit inside their mouths. Once, an African bullfrog ate seventeen young cobras, one after another.

Some frogs seek out their food. A toad hops around after dark, snapping up moths, beetles, and crickets. It may eat more than 5,000 insects during a single summer. Other frogs ambush their prey. A horned frog hides among leaves the rain forest floor in South America. It stays absolutely still, day after day. When an animal comes by, the frog watches attentively, waiting until it moves closer. Then it seizes the prey with a loud snap of its huge mouth. The horned frog is not a fussy eater. It gulps down cockroaches, lizards, mice, and even other horned frogs.

It is easy to see why some people say that a frog is like a stomach with legs, eyes, and a very big mouth. This horned frog has just swallowed a mouse.

Frogs are prey, too. Birds, snakes, raccoons, and many other animals eat them. That is why many frogs are wonderfully camouflaged in colors of green or brown. When a predator wanders near, a frog will often crouch into its surroundings. It will stay very still and quiet, hoping not to be spotted.

This mossy frog (left) is impossible to spot in the mossy streams of its home in Vietnam. This toad from the Amazon (above) looks just like a dead leaf on the rain forest floor.

Even if a frog is discovered, it still has an escape plan. It can jump. A big bullfrog can jump more than six feet. **As it takes off, powerful muscles straighten the long legs folded under its body.** Its eyes sink into its head for protection, and special see-through "eyelids," called *nictitating membranes*, cover them like safety goggles. After a good leap, the bullfrog splashes into a pond and hides under some waterweeds.

A jumping frog usually stretches out its front legs to absorb the impact of landing.

Some frogs have other ways to foil predators. If the common toad sees a snake, it can puff up its body like a ball so that it looks too big to swallow. Dart poison frogs, as their name tells you, are poisonous. They hop around the rain forest floor, showing off their beautiful colors that warn other animals to stay away. Just one lick can put off a predator for life.

The skin of some dart frogs contains enough poison to kill ten people.

Many colorful dart poison frogs live in the rain forests of Central and South America. Scientists believe they get the poisons in their skin from ants and perhaps other insects they eat.

The gliding frogs of Southeast Asia make the most spectacular escape from predators. The first scientists to discover this frog could hardly believe their eyes. **A gliding frog can leap from the top of a rain forest tree and glide for fifty feet using large webbed feet.** It steers its body through the air to grab the branch of a nearby tree.

Scientists have discovered more than 5,000 types of frogs. Many, like the gliding frog, live in the rain forest. It is always warm and wet there, so it is a perfect environment for them. But some frogs live in dry deserts. How do they manage that?

Gliding frogs have suckers on their toes to grab leaves as they land. If you count, you will see that frogs have only four toes on each front foot.

Spadefoot toads survive in dry places by digging underground to where the soil is more moist. The toads can sleep for weeks until they feel the sound of raindrops falling on the ground above. Then they dig back to the surface at night. It is an amazing event. Hundreds pop out of the earth almost at once, splashing in puddles left by a storm.

The Australian water-holding frog fills its body with water before it burrows into the desert. It sheds layers of old skin to make a protective case called a *cocoon*. This keeps the frog moist so it can survive for months and perhaps even years — if it isn't dug up first. The indigenous peoples of Australia found a way to use these frogs to quench their thirst. They squeezed them gently for a drink and then let them go.

A spadefoot toad can bury itself in seconds by digging with its hind feet. People have found them several feet underground.

Other survival tricks help some kinds of frogs live in very cold places. In winter, these frogs dive to the bottom of ponds and bury themselves in the mud. Some crawl under logs or find burrows for shelter. As it gets colder, they stop moving. Their heartbeats and breathing slow. Sometimes their hearts may stop altogether. A few frogs, such as wood frogs and spring peepers, will even freeze partly solid. They have a sort of antifreeze in their blood that lets them survive.

The wood frog can live in colder places than any other frog in North America. It even survives in Alaska.

30

When spring sunshine warms the ground, a frog's heartbeat and breathing slowly get faster. Then the frog wakes up. Next it is ready for a big event. It joins hundreds of frogs on the move, hopping, leaping, or swimming toward lakes, ponds, or large puddles where they breed. Some frogs may travel more than eight miles to their breeding places.

As soon as they arrive, the male frogs start singing. **Each type of frog has a special call.** It might be a grunt, a croak, or a snort. Some frogs sound like quacking ducks, others like tinkling bells. But they are all saying the same thing. To a female frog, the singing means, "Pick me, pick me!" To another male frog, the singing usually means, "Keep away, keep away!"

After sleeping all winter on the bottom of a pond, a bullfrog will swim to the surface in spring. Then the male frogs will start singing for a mate.

This young toad tadpole has been caught by a giant water bug.

Each male sings to attract a female mate. If she likes his singing, the female may let him fertilize the eggs she lays. For a bullfrog, that could be as many as 20,000 eggs. Other frogs may lay only a handful.

Each egg is surrounded by clear jelly for protection. **The egg hatches into a tadpole, which looks more like a fish than a frog.** It has a head, a tail, and gills for breathing underwater. At first the tadpole may feed on small plants, called *algae*. It has tiny teeth to scrape the algae from rocks and logs.

Bullfrog eggs take about four days to hatch. The dark shapes you see are the developing tadpoles.

When it gets bigger, the tadpole may also eat small animals. It feeds most of the time, and its body starts to change. **Tiny back legs and front legs appear and slowly get bigger.** The tadpole's gills get smaller as lungs develop inside its body. Then it spends more time at the surface, taking gulps of air. Eventually the tadpole stops eating. It absorbs its tail as food, and the tail disappears. Now it looks more like a frog than a tadpole.

As it gets bigger, a bullfrog tadpole will start to use its hind legs for swimming.

These young frogs on a lily pad have come out of the water for the first time. They will soon have to learn to hunt for insects.

A bullfrog tadpole may take two years to turn into a small frog. **Then it crawls out of the water, ready to explore its new surroundings.** The young frog will spend most of its life near big lakes and ponds. Bullfrogs love to hide in the waterweeds and wait to snatch insects.

Other kinds of tadpoles may turn into frogs in just a month or two. Wood frogs, toads, and spring peepers often breed in small ponds and pools that can dry out. So their tadpoles have to grow up and leave their home before it disappears. When they are ready, they hop away to live in nearby fields and forests.

Tadpoles and small frogs are always in danger. Water beetles, fish, birds, and even other frogs eat them. So it is no surprise that some frogs look after their young. **The African bullfrog fiercely defends its eggs and tadpoles.** It will try to scare away people, and even lions, that get too close.

Other frogs are even more amazing parents. The marsupial frog from South America protects its eggs and tadpoles inside a special pouch, like a kangaroo. The gastric brooding frog of Australia swallows her eggs. The tadpoles grow in the safety of her stomach for about two months. Then with a hiccup, they hop out.

Strawberry dart poison frogs are probably the hardest-working parents of all. The female lays her eggs on the damp rain forest floor instead of in a pond. When a tadpole hatches, it wriggles onto the mother's back and she carries it up into a tree. There, she looks for a plant called a *bromeliad*, which holds pools of water between its leaves, and that is where she puts her tadpole. Then she goes down to fetch her other tadpoles and puts each in a different bromeliad pool.

She will climb back every few days to see each tadpole. If one is hungry, the tadpole does a special wriggle dance. That tells the mother to lay an egg nearby. It is not a fertile egg, so it will not hatch. It is food for her young. She cares for her treetop nurseries for several weeks, until each tadpole has turned into a small frog.

The strawberry dart poison frog from Central America is barely bigger than a bumblebee, yet a female may climb fifty feet up into a tree to tend to its tadpoles. Some types of dart poison frogs are so toxic that indigenous peoples used to wipe their dart tips on the frog's skin to make them deadly.

By the time a tadpole has become a frog it is ready to begin a new life. Young strawberry dart poison frogs will have bright colors just like their parents to protect them from enemies. Young red-eyed tree frogs will have suckers on their toes, like their parents, to climb into trees. They will have large eyes to spot insects, and sticky tongues to catch them. And they will soon know how to hunt for prey and hide from predators.

This young red-eyed tree frog is just half an inch long. It will take many months of hunting and eating for it to grow to adult size, which is two to three inches long.

photo: Vivien Pybus

I love to paddle my canoe through the waterweeds.

I like to watch dragonflies zoom overhead and fish swim in the depths. And best of all, I like to see frogs. Their large bright eyes and engaging faces make them one of my favorite animals.

The months I worked on this book were filled with fun moments. One was trying to photograph the frog catching a caterpillar. At first the frog was too shy to do this in front of the camera. It hid every time it saw the special flash guns, laser trip beams, and other equipment I set up to take the photograph.

So I trained the frog. I first got it to jump for crickets and caterpillars I held with tweezers. Then I slowly put my equipment in place, bit by bit, so the frog was not scared. It took many weeks, but eventually my frog learned to

46

ignore my camera stuff and was happy to leap at anything that looked tasty. It would even go for the tips of my fingers if I didn't watch out. I was able to take lots of photographs so I could get just the right one, and my frog never ran out of an appetite. If you look you can see how full its belly is.

I also had fun looking after some of the frogs in this book at home. I reared them from babies, until they were big enough to photograph. A few, like my gliding frogs, are now favorite pets. They wake me some nights with their gentle singing.

Many other frogs were found by exploring the ponds and swamps near my home. I spent many days searching in the cattails. I also visited rain forests, where many frogs look as if they have just leapt off the page of a storybook. Some things were amazing, like the colors of dart poison frogs, as tiny as jelly beans on the forest floor. One wonderful night, I watched red-eyed tree frogs moving as carefully as tightrope walkers through the treetops.

I had surprises, too. Once, I jumped when a piece of wood hopped from under my feet and turned into a toad, unlike any I had seen before. But my favorite rain forest surprise was the glass frog. It was as small as a pea, with thin legs and delicate toes. You can imagine my excitement when I photographed its underside. I could see the glass frog's organs

Nic and one of his gliding frogs.

and even its tiny heart, beating inside its body. It looked as detailed as the insides of a wristwatch.

Index

Entries in **bold** indicate photographs.

Glossary

Amphibian A type of animal that usually has gills and lives in water when young, and breathes air and lives on land when adult.

Antifreeze A substance that lowers the temperature at which water freezes.

Oxygen A gas in the air that animals need to live.

Environment The conditions that surround a living thing and affect its survival.

Indigenous peoples The original people who lived in a region or those who have lived there since earliest historical times.

Predator An animal that lives by hunting other animals for food.

Prey An animal that is hunted by another animal for food.